Next-Generation Communication

Combining Virtual Reality and Social Media

Table of Contents

Chapter 1. Introduction

The dawn of a new era in communication is upon us, taking the shape of an extraordinary merger of Virtual Reality (VR) and Social Media. In our Special Report, we unveil the remarkable potential of fusing these two technologies together. "Next-Generation Communication: Combining Virtual Reality and Social Media" explores this burgeoning phenomenon that's set to redefine the communication landscape. This comprehensive report isn't a dense technical manifesto; rather it's an exciting, accessible, and enlightening journey through the most advanced technological development of our time. Allow us to escort you into this brave new world where communication is immersive, interactive, and astonishingly real. Now is the time to invest in foresight - this Special Report is your ticket!

Chapter 2. The Genesis of Virtual Reality and Social Media

To fully appreciate the fusion of Virtual Reality (VR) and social media, we must first understand their origins.

2.1. The Genesis of Virtual Reality (VR)

Virtual Reality, the manifestation of computer-generated three-dimensional environments, was not birthed overnight. Its conceptual origins date back to the early 20th century. Despite being a term of contemporary fame, its roots take us back to "Pygmalion's Spectacles," a short story written by science-fiction author Stanley G. Weinbaum in 1936. It suggested a concept where a person could experience a synthetic world through holographic, touch, taste, and smell sensations—a theme central to the modern understanding of VR.

Fast-forward to 1965, computer scientist Ivan Sutherland, in his essay "The Ultimate Display", envisioned a world where users could "look at" a virtual world as if it was reality—kineticizing the concept of VR.

In 1968, Sutherland and his student, Bob Sproull, created "Sword of Damocles," the first head-mounted display (HMD) system for immersive simulation. Although primitive—hanging from the laboratory ceiling—this invention sparked the VR movement.

Through the 1980s and 1990s, VR stepped out of the realms of academic research and began to shape commercial aspirations. Jaron Lanier, credited with popularizing the term "Virtual Reality," founded

VPL Research to develop and market VR gear. However, due to the constraints of available computing technology at the time, quality VR experiences remained elusive.

In 2010, a significant turn came in VR history with Palmer Luckey's creation of the "Oculus Rift," arousing massive public interest. Oculus VR was soon absorbed by social media giant Facebook for approximately $2 billion in 2014, signaling their faith in VR as a next-generation communication platform.

Throughout these stages, VR has oscillated between being a distant hallucination and a palpable transformation of human experiences. Today, as we slide the visor over our heads, reaching out to touch and manipulate digital renderings with tangible feedback, the dreams of the likes of Sutherland and Lanier have finally been realized.

2.2. The Genesis of Social Media

The birth of social media is a topic of much debate, with many tracing its origins back to bulletin board systems (BBS) and Internet Relay Chat (IRC) around the late 1970s and 1980s. These communication platforms permitted users to share information, messages, and even files over raw and decentralized networks.

The arrival of Six Degrees, recognized as the first social networking site, upturned the game. Launched in 1997, it enabled users to create profiles, connect with others, and post bulletin board-like messages. While the site didn't survive the dot-com crash, it triggered the onset of the social media movement.

Years later, Friendster emerged in 2002, followed by MySpace in 2003, further popularizing social networking. On the other hand, LinkedIn, primarily targeting professionals, deployed a more sober approach to social networking in 2003.

However, the seismic shift in the social media landscape came with the genesis of Facebook in 2004. Hacked together in a Harvard dorm room by Mark Zuckerberg and his friends, Facebook rapidly expanded from a college-only network to a global phenomenon. Today, serving 2.85 billion monthly active users (as of June 2021), Facebook reigns over the social media kingdom.

In parallel, platforms including YouTube, Twitter, Instagram, Snapchat, and TikTok added to the social media pantheon, each offering unique ways of user interaction and expression, forming an integral part of our digital lives.

2.3. Fusing VR and Social Media

The histories of VR and social media seem to run on parallel tracks, with both aiming to bring people closer together, albeit with different mechanisms. Today, these paths converge as we stand on the precipice of an era where VR and social media coalesce to create a more compelling, communal, and immersive communication tool.

Although this nascent fusion of VR and social media is still evolving, platforms like Facebook Horizon and VRChat are testing this cosmic blend, giving users a glimpse into an enthralling future where we'll experience, instead of just communicating with, the digital world.

In this report, we stride onward, holding your hand as we plunge deeper into this revolution, a crucial manifestation of a larger shift: the Digital Renaissance. The evolution of VR and social media paints a vibrant picture of our shared digital destiny. Their merger might just redefine the way humans communicate and relate to each other for generations to come.

Chapter 3. The Convergence: VR and Social Media

In the digital age, we've seen an evolution of platforms designed to connect people across distances and share information instantaneously. From the era of emails and newsgroups to the innovation of social networking platforms, the landscape of communication has continuously advanced. However, nothing is perhaps more exciting and transformative than the convergence of VR technology and social media.

3.1. The Transformation of Communication

Communication as we know it has been continually reshaped by technology. In its most primitive forms, communication was limited to face-to-face interactions, handwritten letters, and eventually, to telegraph and telephone. With the advent of the internet, we gifted ourselves with an entirely new paradigm. Websites, emails, instant messengers, and social networks gave birth to an era of instantaneous mass communication - an era where we remained connected despite physical distances.

Now, another innovative leap awaits us. The next evolutionary progression of communication technology promises not just to augment our reality, but to provide an entirely new medium for our experiences and interactions. The key lies in the merging of VR (Virtual Reality) with social media platforms.

3.2. The Power of Virtual Reality

Virtual Reality isn't a new concept. Tractable back to the 1960s, VR's practical introduction to society has been relatively recent, primarily in the form of immersive gaming and training simulations. In essence, VR technology immerses the user into a simulated reality – creating convincing, interactive 3D environments through a combination of audio, video, and haptic feedback.

At the forefront, VR is designed to induce a sense of presence - the feeling of "being there" in the virtual environment. By tricking our perceptions, VR allows us to explore and interact with digital spaces as if they were real. The prospect of using this technology to rethink the norms of communication is tantalizing.

3.3. The Emergence of Social VR

Over the past few years, the symbiosis between VR and social media has started to become clearer. With the rise of platforms like Facebook Spaces (now renamed Horizon), Rec Room, and AltspaceVR, the concept of Social VR–VR applications designed for social interactions–is gradually transitioning from a futuristic concept into a present reality.

In these Social VR spaces, users are represented by customizable avatars, effectively providing a digital embodiment. Beyond mere text-based messages or voice and video calls, users can interact in three-dimensional environments, share digital content, and carry out actions as though they were interacting in the physical world.

3.4. The Influence of Major Tech Companies

Both major industry players like Facebook and startups alike are pioneering in Social VR technology. Facebook, for example, rebranded itself as Meta Platforms Inc., a symbolic gesture towards its ambition of creating a 'metaverse', an online world where people can game, work, and communicate in a VR environment.

Similarly, developments by other companies, such as Microsoft's acquisition of AltspaceVR, suggests a broader industry trend towards embracing VR as a new frontier of social interaction.

3.5. Social VR: A Closer Look

The attractions of Social VR are multifold. For one, it offers a more immersive social experience than any other digital platform. It opens up new possibilities for how people connect, interact, share experiences, and express themselves. Furthermore, it provides a new avenue for virtual communities, social events, and collaborative activities.

In AltspaceVR, for instance, users can gather to play games, watch films, attend live comedy shows, academic lectures, or even yoga classes. Likewise, Horizon allows users to design and construct their own VR environments, shared spaces where friends can meet and interact.

3.6. Future Prospects: The Social VR Ecosystem

The immediate future of Social VR looks promising and is likely to have far-reaching effects on how we communicate. As VR technology matures and becomes more commonplace, it's expected that existing social media networks will further integrate VR features, enabling increasingly immersive and interactive social experiences.

Education, tourism, work, gaming, and entertainment - it's hard to find an area that couldn't be positively impacted by the integration of Social VR. As tech giants and startups continue to invest and innovate in this space, we are edging closer to an era of transformative digital experiences.

3.7. Conclusion

The convergence of VR and social media reshapes the way we perceive digital communication. By offering enthralling, immersive experiences, Social VR takes us a step closer to bridging the gap between digital and physical interactions.

There remain challenges to overcome – technological, social, and ethical – but as VR technology continues to evolve, we move toward an era where reality is not just enhanced but redefined. We stand at the precipice of a world where our online social architectures not only imitate life but become a thriving reality. This is not just the frontier of communication, but the gateway to a new reality. This is the dawn of Social VR. Let us wait and watch the sun rise.

Chapter 4. The Technical Trailblazers: Key Innovations in VR and Social Media

Virtual Reality (VR) and social media are advancing at an unprecedented pace, both independently and as a combined entity. Innovations by trailblazing technologists in these fields are paving the way for an enthralling and immersive communication experience for users worldwide.

4.1. The Genesis of Virtual Reality

Virtual reality's roots trace back to the 1960s, when a device named 'The Sword of Damocles' was introduced by Ivan Sutherland and his student Bob Sproull. Albeit crude by modern standards, this device offered a glimpse into the virtual world, producing a holographic overlay of a room's wireframe using head-mounted goggles. Today, this basic concept has evolved exponentially, resulting in intricate ecosystems where virtual and physical realities coexist.

The real quantum leap for VR came with the advent of more affordable headsets, such as the Samsung Gear VR and the Google Cardboard. Today, providers like Oculus and HTC Vive offer high-end experiences, while PlayStation VR brings virtual reality to gamers across the globe.

4.2. Virtual Reality: Key Innovations

Several key innovations are consistently refining VR to deliver engaging and immersive experiences.

Eye-tracking technology has significantly advanced VR experiences.

It increases immersion by simulating natural eye movements within the virtual environment, creating a deeper sense of realism. This technology also allows for 'foveated rendering', whereby resolution is highest at the point where the user is looking, thus optimising graphical performance.

Haptics, another critical innovation, makes the virtual world interactive and tangible. It enables users to touch and manipulate virtual objects, by replicating physical sensations such as pressure, vibrations and even temperature.

Wireless systems eliminate the need for complex, restrictive cabling systems, thereby enhancing the freedom and versatility of user movements.

The current innovation wave includes **virtual smell and taste**, hinting at 'full sensory' virtual environments in the future, although we are still in the nascent stages of these technologies.

4.3. Evolution of Social Media

Before the turn of the century, social media wasn't even a term in the popular lexicon. The advent of platforms like SixDegrees and Friendster laid the groundwork, but it was the emergence of Facebook, YouTube, Twitter and others that caused a seismic shift in interpersonal communication.

Fast forward to today, social media has proliferated into nearly every aspect of our lives and continues to evolve. Instagram's visual storytelling, Snapchat's ephemeral content, and LinkedIn's professional network are examples of how social media is constantly redefining itself.

4.4. Social Media: Key Innovations

Tectonic shifts in the social media landscape have been spurred by numerous innovations.

Mobile technology has arguably been the most influential. The ubiquity of smartphones and the advent of app-based platforms have made social media a constant companion for people worldwide.

The emergence of **live streaming** features on platforms like Facebook and Twitter (Periscope) has enabled real-time sharing of events, further bridging the gap between online and offline worlds.

Augmented Reality (AR) filters in Snapchat and Instagram are pushing the boundaries of user-generated content, making social more interactive and fun.

Artificial intelligence and machine learning are used extensively for targeted advertising, fostering engagement, and enhancing user experience with chatbots and recommendation algorithms.

Integrated **e-commerce features** like Instagram Shop and Facebook Marketplace demonstrate how social platforms are becoming an integral part of the online buying journey.

4.5. The Intersection of VR and Social Media

With VR's immersive capabilities and social media's broad outreach, their fusion is creating an exciting new paradigm. Platforms like vTime and Rec Room are leading this convergence, offering VR-based social networking experiences.

The merge of these two technologies heralds countless opportunities for radical improvements in communication, storytelling, and shared experiences, from virtual meetings to social VR games, enhancing our digital interactions and driving user engagement onto new, thrilling levels.

As we close this chapter, it's apparent that we're on the brink of groundbreaking innovation in both technologies. Tech trailblazers are committed to breaking down existing barriers, fostering a path for enhanced, intricate, and immersive communication methods. A promising road lies ahead for the VR-social media meridian. We just need to stay tuned.

These innovations and more are set to redefine the trajectory of communication technology, making the VR-social media blend not just an exciting prospect but a crucial part of our digital future.

Chapter 5. Revolutionizing Communication: Unpacking the Potential

In the last decade, the evolution of communication has accelerated at an incredible speed, leading to the advent of global communication platforms and immersive interaction experiences unfathomable just a few years ago. Driven by advancements in virtual reality and social media, these technologies' convergence promises a revolution that will redefine human communication.

5.1. From Smoke Signals to Virtual Reality

Understanding the potential held by the integration of VR and social media requires a brief revisit to the evolution of human communication. From prehistoric cave paintings and smoke signals to the written word, electric telegraph, telephone, and now the internet, our means of connecting with one another has continually adapted to the demands and possibilities of our circumstances.

The relatively recent invention of social media has drastically changed communication, reducing physical distances to nothing by providing real-time, widespread interaction. Imagine the next step, where we break free from the constraints of text and video, entering a new dimension made possible by virtual reality (VR) technology: a space where we can meet, talk, and share experiences as if we were in the same room.

5.2. The Tale of Two Technologies

Virtual Reality (VR) and Social Media are two powerful, transformative forces in communication technology. VR offers users an immersive, interactive experience within a simulated environment, while Social Media allows people to connect, interact, and share content across vast geographic distances.

The marriage of these technologies opens doors to a new era of communication, where interactions are not just global but also immersive and sensorially rich. Imagine a world where you can attend international conferences from your living room, explore new destinations virtually with friends, or even hold interactive training sessions with colleagues around the globe.

5.3. Immersive Dimensions of Socializing

The fusion of VR and social media offers immense possibilities for social interaction. Platforms like Facebook's Horizon Workrooms or Oculus Venues allow users to create avatars and explore digital environments, engage in group activities, and interact with others as if they're physically present.

It promises the hyper-realistic integration of sight, sound, and even tactile sensations, which can transform remote communication. People might not just hear and see their interlocutor but could shake hands, hug or feel the ambiance of a shared digital environment. This depth of interaction transcends mere novelty; it could redefine how we perceive presence and connection in a digital world.

5.4. A New Era for Business Communication

The convergence of these technologies could also offer substantial benefits to businesses in terms of training, collaboration, and customer service. A VR-social media platform could transform remote work, providing a virtual office that team members from across the world can tap into. This shared digital environment can closely mimic a physical workspace, complete with meeting rooms, whiteboards, and water coolers, ensuring colleagues can collaborate effectively.

Similarly, this amalgamation could revolutionize customer communication. Businesses could offer virtual reality tours of their facilities, let customers try products virtually, or offer immersive, interactive customer support.

5.5. Hurdles and Considerations

Despite the exciting potential of VR-social media convergence, there are also challenges and risks to consider. These include tech accessibility, privacy, and mental health concerns. A significant portion of the world's population might not have the necessary resources to access VR technology. There are also concerns about personal privacy in an even more interconnected and potentially less anonymous world. Plus, there's the risk of 'digital overdose' as users could end up spending an unhealthy amount of time in VR environments, which could impact psychological health.

5.6. A Leap into Tomorrow

The idea of integrating VR with Social Media is still relatively new, and the true potential of this fusion remains to be discovered. Undeniably, it's a thrilling step forward into a future of communication that only a short time ago resided within the realms of science fiction.

Throughout history, each significant shift in communication has been met with skepticism and apprehension alongside excitement and exhilaration. The blending of VR and social media will likely follow the same path. As we find ways to navigate the challenges and grasp the opportunities offered by this new era of communication, we edge closer to a future where connection and presence extend beyond the physical world.

By integrating the immersive experience of virtual reality with the globally linked realms of social media, we immerse ourselves not just in a different reality, but a new era of communication. As the potential of this collaboration unfolds, individuals and businesses alike should stay attuned to possibilities, adapt flexibly, and evolve adeptly in order to harness the opportunities this revolution offers.

Such is the thrilling, transformative promise of this moment: a step forward into a world where communication is not just about exchanging information, but about shared, immersive, multi-sensory experiences that bridge the physical and digital domains in unprecedented ways.

Chapter 6. Advancements in Immersive Experiences

The immersive landscape has experienced a rapid technological leap, fueled by the advent of Virtual Reality (VR) and Augmented Reality (AR) technologies. From creating fully immersive games to virtual tours and simulations, these technologies allow users to interact and navigate through three-dimensional spheres, blurring the line between what's virtual and what's real.

6.1. The Journey of Immersive Experiences

The history of immersive experiences maps a fascinating journey. Initially, it consisted of rudimentary computer-generated animations that left a lot to the imagination. As the years passed, and technology progressed, we saw the advent of more complex immersive experiences, featuring captivating graphics and interactive interfaces. This evolution laid the foundation for Virtual Reality, which opened a door into a world of ground-breaking immersive experiences.

6.2. The Evolution of Virtual Reality

Once confined to the corners of science fiction, VR has now become an intrinsic part of our reality. The 21st-century marks an era of considerable change in the technological landscape. This transformation was powered by giants like Oculus, Sony, and HTC debuting their VR headsets, presenting user interactions that were hitherto just mere propositions.

6.3. The Rise of Augmented Reality

Mirroring the rise of VR, Augmented Reality (AR) has also grown exponentially. The inception of AR technology can be traced back to heads-up displays (HUDs) in military airplanes. However, the most significant zeitgeist moment that propelled the AR technology into mainstream consciousness was the release of Pokemon Go. This simple yet addictive game demonstrated the amusement that can be derived from AR and left a profound influence on how we understand immersive experiences.

6.4. The Impact of Technology on Immersive Experiences

Developments in hardware, software, and network capabilities have substantially amplified the quality of immersive experiences. Faster processors offer more real-time rendering, while high-resolution displays provide crisp visuals. Advances in tracking systems allow for precise user interactions, and improvements in haptic feedback provide a realistic sense of touch.

6.5. Mainstream Adoption of VR and AR Experiences

The adoption of immersive experiences is no longer restricted to the gaming industry or niche technology enthusiasts. Industries such as real estate, healthcare, education, and tourism employ VR and AR for creating interactive experiences that transcend geographical boundaries.

6.6. The Role of Social Media in Immersive Experiences

Social media has had a profound influence on VR and AR adoption. Platforms like Facebook, Instagram, and Snapchat have integrated AR filters, allowing users to create and share personalized immersive experiences. Social VR platforms, such as AltspaceVR and VRChat, allow users to create avatars, visit virtual environments, and interact with others, thereby translating social networking into a three-dimensional, interactive experience.

6.7. The Future of Immersive Experiences

The future of immersive experiences is promising and continually evolving. The interplay of VR and Social Media has the potential to reinvent our perceptions of reality. This merger will foster a new generation of experiences that are more engaging, interactive, and social.

6.8. Challenges and Potential Solutions

Despite the prospects, the road to the widespread adoption of immersive experiences is not devoid of challenges. Issues such as motion sickness, privacy concerns, and the high cost of devices thwart mass accessibility. However, with continuous advancements, potential solutions are on the horizon which could mitigate these challenges and pave the way for even more immersive and engaging experiences.

Diving into the immersive world has never been more exciting. Having traversed the transformational journey of VR and AR, it's intriguing to imagine what the future of these technologies holds. The incredible potential points towards a horizon beyond imagination, harnessing the power of technology to redefine the very concept of experience. Life is becoming not just about being a passive observer but an active participant in interactive landscapes that resonate on personal, social, and professional levels. A new era of communication is upon us, mixing Virtual Reality and Social Media in ways that will redefine the landscape of interaction.

Chapter 7. The Social Media Metaverse: A Deeper Dive

In the ever-evolving digital world, two seemingly disparate platforms have intersected, promising a transformative leap in how we communicate and socialize online. As you journey through this chapter, you'll discover how the innovation dubbed 'The Social Media Metaverse' has been spurred by the fusion of Virtual Reality (VR) and Social Media.

7.1. VR and Social Media: Unprecedented Alliance

The unexpected synergy between VR and Social Media was not immediately apparent. Yet, with the growth of VR technologies and the ubiquitous influence of social media platforms, an integrative vision emerged. The first hint came through demand for more immersive digital experiences, driven by a user base seeking more engaging, human-like interactions. Simultaneously, advancements in VR technology began to facilitate incredibly immersive, real-world experiences. The intersection of these two trends instigated the creation of the Social Media Metaverse.

7.2. Defining the Social Media Metaverse

The 'Social Media Metaverse' is a term born out of necessity to describe a revolutionary blend of VR and social media. Technically, it refers to a collective virtual shared space, including the sum of all virtual worlds, augmented reality, and the Internet. But the metaverse is not just a technical term; it epitomizes the future of digital experiences, where users can interact with a computer-generated environment and other users in real-time.

7.3. Navigating the Social Media Metaverse

Imagine logging in to your favorite Social Media site, but instead of scrolling through a news feed, you find yourself in a virtual environment, interacting with friends' avatars. That's the most basic experience the Social Media Metaverse offers. Users can participate in interactive gameplay, join communities, attend virtual concerts or meetings, even own virtual real estate – making every online interaction more engaging and memorable than ever.

7.4. The Impact of The Social Media Metaverse on Social interactions

The Social Media Metaverse transcends the boundary separating digital and physical interactions. It brings with it a new suite of emotive expression tools, extending beyond emojis and stickers to VR gestures capable of mimicking real-life human interactions. Conversations in social media's metaverse will be more immersive, personal, and interactive. Owing to 'presence,' the psychological phenomenon elicited by VR technology, users may feel as though they are truly with their interlocutors, sculpting a whole new layer of empathy and depth to online communication.

7.5. Technological Requirements and Challenges

Creating a seamless, immersive social media metaverse isn't a simple feat, and numerous technological and ethical challenges need addressing. High-resolution VR headsets, robust tracking systems, and massive data processing capabilities are crucial for powering these unique experiences. Security and privacy also emerge as prominent concerns, requiring stringent data encryption and anonymization methods to protect user identity and safeguard interactions.

7.6. Market Penetration and Future Scope

VR technology and social media are already widely adopted across the global population, yet the pinnacle of their fusion – the metaverse – is still in its nascent stage. As of today, a handful of tech behemoths like Meta (previously Facebook) have expressed interest in pushing forward the idea of the Social Media Metaverse with varying degrees of success. However, wider adoption is expected in the coming decade as the technology matures, prices decrease, and more innovative use-cases emerge.

7.7. Conclusion

The Social Media Metaverse anticipates a future where digital and physical realities converge, utterly revolutionizing our concept of online interaction. This chapter propels you into this future, elucidating the extraordinary potential of VR and Social Media synergy. This amalgamation will soon redefine the current communication landscape, offering immersive, interactive, and astonishingly 'real' experiences. However, this inevitable transition will necessitate careful and considered navigation to ensure the development of a digital era that offers increased engagement and connection while preserving user safety and privacy.

Chapter 8. Next-Gen Connectivity: Benefits and Opportunities

Contextualizing The Technological Leap ===

From handwritten letters to emails, from telegrams to instant messaging – the evolution of communication has been remarkable. When paired with social media, the advancements have successfully bridged geographical distances, allowing people to stay connected through shared posts, direct messages, and online hangouts. Now, an unprecedented shift is emerging as Virtual Reality (VR) brings an unparalleled level of immersion to this landscape.

Join us as we undress this exciting fusion and delve into its plethora of benefits and opportunities.

VR and Social Media: A Commendable Confluence ===

Virtual Reality, equipped with headsets and motion sensors, allows users to be part of a simulated 3D environment. Social media, on the other hand, has become the modern town square - a space where people interact, share ideas, and forge connections.

The combination of VR and social media can create a revolutionary platform, enabling real-time, immersive communication experiences that are more engaging and interactive. Picture having a heart-to-heart conversation with a friend seated right across from you in a cozy digital café, despite being thousands of miles apart in the physical world. Imagine the thrill of watching your favorite music band perform live with fellow enthusiasts, all in the digital comfort of your own space. This is the new wave that VR and social media integration is about to unleash.

Unfolding Benefits ===

The blend of VR and social media yields several immense benefits.

Entertainment Amplified

Beyond gaming applications, the merging of VR and social media provides a game-changing entertainment platform. Users can enjoy live concerts, sports events, and autonomous entertainment experiences in 3D environments with their friends, irrespective of their geographical locations.

Real-Time Collaborative Workspaces

Enterprises can build immersive, interactive workspaces where employees can collaborate in real-time from distant locations – a vital benefit, especially considering the rising trend of remote work. These virtual social spaces can stimulate brainstorming sessions, trainings, and meetings in a more engaging manner.

Empathetic Communication

Users can transmit non-verbal cues such as body language and gestures, enhancing the ability to empathize and connect with others on a deeper level than through any other digital platform. This empathetic connection could boost social media's user engagement and user experience.

Immersive Learning Experiences

VR-powered social media platforms can offer experiential learning opportunities. These can range from virtual field trips to simulated practical experiments, making learning more interactive and fun.

Assessing Opportunities ===

Capitalizing on the benefits mentioned above, several opportunities are waiting to be explored.

Retail Market

In a virtual marketplace, customers can have a more realistic examination of the product, engaging all their senses prior to purchase. The application of VR in social e-commerce will undoubtedly boost the user's online shopping experience.

Healthcare Sector

With VR-powered social platforms, therapists can provide treatment in a more interactive manner, and patients can join support groups without the need to step out from their homes, breaking down geographical barriers.

Virtual Tourism

Tourism enterprises could offer virtual tours of exotic places, museums, or historical sites. This would allow people to explore the world together with their friends or relatives, right from their living room.

Corporate Trainings

Employee training can be enhanced by utilizing VR-powered social platforms. They present the opportunity to create immersive and engaging training programs, aiding employees to pick up new skills or procedures in a hands-on manner.

Real Estate Industry

A virtual tour of a house or an apartment would ease the home-buying process. It can help potential buyers make quicker, more informed decisions.

Taking The Leap Ahead ===

Mashing up VR with social media is not a mere mix of technologies but a game-changing revolution in the offing. The potential benefits and opportunities are endless, and the technological leap promises to overhaul conventional communication norms. It declares a world where communication isn't confined to texts or voice calls; it's immersive, real, and breathtaking.

While embarking on this ameliorating journey, it is crucial to be mindful of the challenges - be it ensuring data privacy, managing potential cyber threats, or creating inclusive and accessible experiences. While we explore the untapped, it is equally critical to address these issues proactively.

A well-calibrated integration of VR and social media sits on the horizon, pledging to revolutionize the way we communicate, work, play, learn, and connect. The virtual realm is reaching out to us, and it is time for us to embrace this boundless expanse of possibilities.

Chapter 9. Challenges and Overcoming Limitations

While the merger of Virtual Reality (VR) and Social Media represents an exciting avenue for the future of communication, it is not without its challenges and limitations. In this chapter, we explore these issues in detail and uncover solutions to transform these hurdles into stepping stones leading us to the next dimension of communication.

9.1. Technological Limitations

High-quality VR demands high-performance hardware. The implementation of VR in social media requires considerable computational power and high-speed internet. Moreover, a powerful graphics processing unit (GPU) is essential to render virtual environments in real time.

In terms of hardware, VR headsets are still evolving. The need for more comfortable, lightweight hardware that offers high-definition visuals and high-fidelity audio poses a significant challenge.

Overcoming these limitations requires advancements in the technology itself. Companies such as NVIDIA are investing heavily in GPU, optimizing hardware for VR. Tech giants like Facebook are also investing in the evolution of VR headsets.

9.2. Accessibility and Affordability

High-end VR systems are costly, which limits their accessibility for many people around the world. The high-speed internet required for smooth functioning can additionally increase costs.

Companies focused on VR are tackling this by introducing more affordable alternatives. Standalone VR headsets have started to emerge, offering a more cost-effective solution. Governments and telecommunications companies worldwide need to invest in high-speed internet infrastructure to make high-speed internet more affordable and accessible.

9.3. Health Concerns

Health concerns are another area of challenge. Prolonged use of VR can lead to cybersickness, a state marked by symptoms akin to motion sickness. Prolonged exposure to VR systems may also impact posture and eye health.

Overcoming these concerns requires additional research and technological solutions. Options like implementing a "safety virtual space" and creating visual indicators within the VR environment for users taking prolonged sessions have been suggested.

9.4. Privacy and Data Security

The marriage of VR and social media also poses privacy and data security concerns. As communications get more immersive, they also become more intimate. Social media platforms will have to reckon with the additional data that they can potentially collect and the privacy implications therein.

To mitigate these issues, stringent data policies are required. Legislation akin to GDPR in Europe could be implemented to protect user data. Anonymization techniques could also be used to anonymize the data collected to prevent misuse.

9.5. User Adaptation

The transition from traditional social media platforms to VR-based platforms will require time and user adaptation. User comfort with VR tools, navigating virtual environments, and communication etiquette in VR are a few areas that require understanding and acclimation.

The challenge of user adaptation can be addressed through training, tutorial videos, and intuitive design of virtual spaces. Also, the gradual introduction of VR aspects in social media platforms can ease the transition.

9.6. Content Creation

The true potential of VR would be fully realized when users can not only consume content but also create their own VR spaces and share with others. This demands easy to use VR content creation tools.

Overcoming this challenge will require tech firms to invest in user-friendly, versatile VR content creation software. Training and support will also be crucial in empowering users to set off on their own VR encounters.

While the hurdles are manifold, overcoming them, led by technological advancements and prompted by necessity, we are undoubtedly on the precipice of a new era. In the ensuing sections, we will explore further facets of VR and Social Media fusion, showcasing potential use-cases and future implications. The confluence of these technologies holds an exciting future, promising a breathtaking revolution in the realm of communication.

Chapter 10. The Future Forecast: Analysts' Perspectives

As we gaze into the crystal globe of the future, the blending of Virtual Reality (VR) and Social Media creates exciting possibilities. Amid the hustle of technological advancement, analysts ponder what this merger will mean for users, industries, and society as a whole. Their perspectives offer compelling insights that paint a vibrant picture of the future.

10.1. The Evolving User Experience

Pioneering advancements in VR technology coupled with increasing integration into social media platforms will undoubtedly redefine the digital user experience. Analysts anticipate that we will transition from passive scrolling and swiping to active participation within digital spaces, facilitated by VR. Users can expect more immersive and interactive experiences, resulting in heightened emotional engagement with content and deeper social connections. The digital social experience will evolve from being an extension of our physical world to becoming a distinctive realm with its own nuances and possibilities.

10.2. Transforming Social Interactions and Connectivity

Just as smartphones transformed communication earlier this century, the amalgamation of VR and social media is poised to catapult us into a new dimension of connectivity. Experts envisage complete communication circles where voice, video, text, and emotive expressions will be seamlessly integrated, fostering rich, in-depth conversations and connections. Emojis and text messages will give way to communicating with 'presence' and full-fledged avatars, redefining how we express ourselves and connect with others online.

10.3. Empowered Content Creation and Sharing

Current usage of social media primarily involves the consumption of content created by others. The integration of VR may transform consumers into creators, enabling them to design their own social scenarios and experiences in the virtual world. As analysts predict, users will shift from posting pictures and videos to sharing experiences and invitations to their VR spaces. The dynamics of content creation and sharing will witness dramatic changes.

10.4. Impact on Industries

The envisioned integration will dramatically reshape various industries. In the realm of advertising, native ads may be replaced by immersive brand experiences. In education, virtual field trips and labs could supplement traditional teaching methods. Healthcare could benefit from simulated surgeries for training, telerehabilitation, and remote diagnosis. Real estate tours could transition online, with customers being able to virtually inhabit and modify properties. E-commerce could provide a 'try before you buy' experience, reducing returns and increasing customer satisfaction.

10.5. Opportunities and Challenges

With grand opportunities come significant challenges. Privacy and security concerns, for instance, will escalate with the increase in shared and created content. Regulatory frameworks will need to be updated, and ethical questions surrounding virtual behavior will need to be addressed. Digital wellness is another critical aspect, with current research highlighting potential psychological impacts of extensive immersion in virtual environments. However, should these challenges be overcome, the rewards could be revolutionary.

10.6. The Analysts' Verdict

While no one can predict the future with absolute certainty, the consensus among analysts seems to be that the marriage between VR and social media represents a quantum leap in technological advancement. It promises to revolutionize all sectors, from communication and commerce to education and entertainment, making our digital lives more immersive, interactive, and exciting. Indeed, the future is not just about being 'connected' — it's about experiencing connectivity.

In essence, analysts perceive a future studded with digitally-immersed societies, bustling with rich and varied experiences unfathomable by today's standards. With virtual reality and social media spearheading this shift, they compel us to ask not 'if' but 'when' and 'how' the described future will turn into reality. Together, these perspectives sketch a fascinating tableau of a future waiting to unfold. Be it bright or fraught with challenges, one thing remains certain: it will be anything but dull.

Chapter 11. Cultural Shifts and Societal Impact

Over the course of human history, revolutionary technologies have catalyzed societal and cultural shifts of epic proportions. The advent of the written word expanded the human capacity for record-keeping and knowledge dissemination. The invention of the printing press further democratized access to information and brought about the renaissance. More recently, the internet and mobile technology have reshaped global communication irreversibly. At each of these junctions, society has adapted, embraced the new reality, and often flourished because of it. Today, we find ourselves on the precipice of one such transformative technology revolution: The fusion of Virtual Reality (VR) and Social Media.

11.1. A New Medium for Communication

The integration of VR and social media signals the dawn of a new medium, and accordingly, a radical change in the way humans communicate. Suddenly, standard text conversations are augmented with 3D-interactive environments. This deep interactivity calls for a new language, similar to how the internet gave rise to emojis, gifs, and memes. Moving beyond text and images, it adds a spatial dimension, allowing users to express themselves through their surroundings, actions, and non-verbal cues.

This change represents a seismic shift from passive consumption to active participation. Users are no longer observers but actors in the narratives they choose to engage with. It challenges old paradigms, inviting everyone to pursue agency, immersion, and a more meaningful connection with others.

11.2. The Democratisation of Presence

Another compelling societal ramification of the merger of VR and social media revolves around the democratisation of presence. The ability to create, engage with, and partake in various environments from the comfort of one's own home levels the accessibility spectrum. As long as individuals have access to a VR-enabled device and an internet connection, geographic, physical, and socioeconomic barriers that typically limit our ability to experience certain locales or occurances are significantly mitigated.

Furthermore, communities marginalized in the physical world, such as those with mobility impairments, stand to gain tremendously from this merger. Inclusion is no longer restricted to the constraints of physical reality, granting individuals opportunities to engage more fully in the social, political, and cultural arenas.

11.3. Redefining Identity and Self-Expression

The merging of VR and social media offers an entirely new realm for identity expression. Users are granted full control over their virtual appearance and environment, providing them with boundless opportunities for personal and artistic expression. It introduces the concept of fluid identity, where users have the freedom to experiment and transform their representation in the virtual world. Simultaneously, it enables anonymity, allowing users who wish to explore different aspects of themselves without fear of judgment or discrimination.

This widespread exploration of identity and self-expression may lead to a more accepting and inclusive society, as interactions become less focused on physical appearances and more on character and creativity. On the flip side, however, such freedom also necessitates careful thought on regulations and the prevention of misuse.

11.4. Impact on Mental Health

Though the implications of integrating VR and social media are vastly positive, it's imperative that we safeguard against potential mental health impacts. Reports of cyber-bullying, addiction, and mental health issues correlated with prolonged use of social media are well-documented. Now, these risks could be amplified within an immersive VR environment.

Creating spaces that allow for positive interaction, ensuring mechanisms of conflict resolution, and fundamentally, establishing a balance between VR usage and maintaining a connection with the physical world, will be key. Proper standards and sensitivities are needed for this new medium to enhance, and not hamper, our societal well-being.

11.5. The Future Of Work And Education

With the ability to create shared online spaces that mimic the vitality of in-person interactions, the integration of VR and social media will drastically redefine the ways we work and learn. Remote work and online education will feel more engaging and the challenges related to isolation and lack of interaction, currently associated with these models, could become obsolete.

Virtual reality offers the potential to level the playing field for talent and educational opportunities. Talent acquisition could be based on skill alone, as geographic boundaries diminish. Similarly, educational resources could be made universally accessible to children across the globe, irrespective of their location or circumstances.

In the coming years, as the blending of VR and social media deepens, we will be challenged and inspired in ways unprecedented. From the assertion of identity to how we engage in civic issues, it will leave no stone unturned. Basking in its potential, we must also keep an open dialogue about the risks and the responsibilities it carries, and establish the compass that will navigate us through this new frontier.